Christian Crackers

Out of the Mouths of Babes

Collected by

PHIL MASON

MONARCH
BOOKS

Mill Hill, London NW7 3SA and Grand Rapids, Michigan 49501

First published by Monarch Books in the UK 1999. This edition 2001.
Concorde House, Grenville Place, Mill Hill, London NW7 3SA.
Published in the USA by Monarch Books 2001.

Distributed by:
UK: STL, PO Box 300, Kingstown Broadway, Carlisle, Cumbria CA3 0QS;
USA: Kregel Publications, PO Box 2607, Grand Rapids, Michigan 49501.

ISBN 1 85424 531 7 (UK)
ISBN 0 8254 5995 8 (USA)

British Library Cataloguing Data
A catalogue record for this book is available from the British Library.

Cartoons by Mike Buecheler

Designed and produced for the publishers by
Gazelle Creative Productions,
Concorde House, Grenville Place, Mill Hill, London NW7 3SA.
Printed in Singapore.

A friend who was minister in a north country church climbed into the pulpit and announced his text.
"Be still and know that I am God."
A small voice piped up at the back of the church, "Is he really God, mummy?"

"Dad, did you go to Sunday School when you were a boy?"

"Yes, my son, I was always sent to Sunday School."

"Well, I think I'm going to quit; it's not doing me any good either."

Sunday School teacher: "What does the story of David and Goliath teach us?" Tommy: "Please, Miss, to duck!"

Little girl, much impressed with the rosy beaming face of her minister: "Do you polish your face with Godshine?"

A small boy returned from Sunday School in tears. When questioned by his mother about his distressed state, he replied tearfully, "Jesus wants me for a sunbeam, but I want to be an engine driver."

9

Small boy to his new baby sister, whom he had been told was a gift from God: "Quick, before you forget, what does God look like?"

A certain bishop had a fondness for using biblical quotations whenever he attended a function. When he was asked to open a new Maternity Home the organizers thought, "Now we have him stumped." After a few well-chosen words, he looked around and added, "I know you are waiting for a quotation, and here it is: 'We shall not all sleep, but we shall all be changed'."

A 102 year-old lady was asked if she had any worries. "Not since I got my eldest son into an old people's home," she replied.

A child on the way home from school decided to stop at the church and have a look around. When he arrived home he told his Grandmother he had been in God's house. "Oh," said Grandma: "And did you see God?". "No," replied the little boy, "but I saw his wife scrubbing the floor."

A little boy once wrote in his essay on 'Lying': "A lie is an abomination unto the Lord but a very present help in trouble."

Two little boys had been having a very serious discussion. Finally, one of them went up to the Sister who worked in the parish and said, "You're not one of them things that goes into the fields to scare the birds, are you?"

When Antonia was six years old she was informed one Sunday that we were going to church. "Why?" she asked. "To learn about God," replied mother. Antonia frowned and complained, "But we do God at school."

A little boy asked his father if he could have a bike. His father had to say no but added. "If you pray hard you may have a little brother to play with soon." The little boy did pray but soon tired of it. Eventually his father took him upstairs and showed him not one, but two little brothers with whom he could play. "Now aren't you glad that you prayed for a little brother?" he said.

"Yes," said the boy doubtfully, "but aren't you glad I stopped praying when I did?"

At a school nativity play, three young children were cast as the kings. Presenting their gifts at the stable, the first said: "Gold", the second: "Myrrh", and the third: "And Frank sent this".

A little girl had been to Sunday School for the first time and was asked by her mother how it compared with her day school. "Oh! I like it much better," she said. "There are no exams there, and at the end you go to heaven instead of the High School."

A mischievous boy was asked by his mother, "How do you expect to get into heaven?" He thought for a moment and said, "Well, I shall just run in and out and keep slamming the door until they say 'for goodness sake come in or stay out', and then I'll go in."

An old lady was walking past a Sunday School when two small boys came out. The first one said to the other "Do you believe in Satan?", and the second boy answered, "No, it's like when they tell you about Santa Claus – it's your father."

A teenage lad in the third year of a comprehensive school was asked by a visitor: "What do you usually do in religious education lessons?" "Wait for them to finish, Sir" came the frank reply.

Asked about one of the
Commandments, one girl wrote:

"Do not admit adultery."

The Sunday School teacher was telling the story of the nativity, and had just finished the part about there being "No room at the inn". A small voice piped up, "I blame Joseph, he should have booked."

On another occasion the teacher was exploring the children's notion of God.
She asked, "Tommy, who is God?"
Six-year-old Tommy furrowed his brows and thought for a moment or two about the question. Suddenly he brightened, and with a grin said:
"I think God is the man who saved the Queen."

Small boy, looking at the sanctuary lamp during a rather long sermon, "Mum, when the light changes to green can we go?"

The daughter of a minister asked her mother:

"Why does Daddy pray to God before he preaches?"

Her mother replied: "He

asks God to help him."

A cloud came over the little girl's face and she said: "Why doesn't he then?"

You can't win 'em all:

Reporting Easter Sunday baptisms at Corby Baptist Church the minister said: "The whole atmosphere of the day was a blessing to all. All, that is except one. The little granddaughter of one of our baptismal candidates said to her mother afterwards, 'I don't like that man!' 'Why ever not?' asked her mother, 'Well,' replied the little girl, 'He tried to drown my Grandma in that pond, and she had her new dress on.'"

One Pentecost Sunday the scripture reading was from Acts Chapter 2: "Tongues of fire sat on each of them." Looking at the bald heads in front of her my little daughter said: "Was their hair burnt off, daddy?"

One day when our son Einar was about four or five years old I took him to church in Trondheim. He was sitting on my knee

when suddenly the priest
appeared in the sanctuary
behind the communion
rails. Einar whispered in
my ear: "That priest has a
play pen too."

The nursery school children were asked to draw pictures of Jesus' birthplace. One of them drew Mary, Joseph, Jesus in the manger and an enormously fat man. The teacher asked the child who the fat man was, and was told, "Oh that's round John Virgin".

At a visitation to a small church in his Diocese of North Carolina, Bishop Robert W Estill decided to underline his talk to the young people about the Good Shepherd. So he found himself, clad in the full regalia of the episcopacy, including the impressive crook, facing the crowd of youngsters.

"Now," he asked. "Do you know who I am?"

After a moment's silence, one child ventured, "Little Bo Peep?"

One of the questions in a religious education exam at a Christian high school was: What does a bishop do?
One child wrote;

"Move diagonally across the board."

A little girl, saying her prayers one night, was heard to finish with the remark, "Please God, take care of yourself, because if owt happens to you we're sunk."

A little girl told her grandmother, "I behaved very well in church today. I even refused a big plate of money that the man offered me."

The rector, on seeing a small boy trying to reach a doorbell, said: "Let me help you, sonny." The rector gave a good ring. The boy looked at him and said: "Now, mister, run like mad."

After being shown photographs of his parents' wedding a small boy said to his father:

"Was that when you got Mummy to come to work for us?"

A very pretty Sunday School teacher asked her class if anyone knew what a miracle was. "Yes," replied one small girl, "I do, my mum says that it will be a miracle if you don't marry our young curate."

A little boy was given two separate shillings by his mother to take to Sunday School, one to put in the collection and the other to buy some sweets on his way home. Skipping along the road he tripped and dropped the coins. One rolled down a nearby drain. The boy looked up to heaven and said, "Sorry, God, there goes your shilling."

A family were looking around a rather dark, imposing-looking church. The child asked: "Mummy, does God live here?" "Yes dear," replied her mother. "Then why doesn't he *move*?" asked the little girl.

One night my family
rattled off all their...
"God bless all my uncles
and aunts." When we

had finished, my son Scott, aged eight, said in his best robot voice: "This has been a recorded message."

A small boy went to church with his Grandma. Grandma knelt down to pray on entry and the little boy knelt beside her. After a few seconds had passed he said: "Who are we hiding from, Grandma?"

I gave my four year old daughter money for sweets and the Chapel collection plate. Seeing her sweets I asked if she had given some money to God. "No," she replied, "He wasn't there."

Minister to little boy: "I hear that God has brought you two lovely twin brothers."
Little boy: "Yes, and what's more, he knows where their school fees will be coming from – I heard Daddy say so."

A grandfather and his little grandson were praying side by side in church. The little boy was muttering in a barely audible voice, so his grandfather said: "Don't mumble, I can't hear a word you're saying." "I'm not talking to you," said the little boy indignantly.

The Reverend Billy Graham tells the story of the time when he arrived in a small town to preach. Wanting to post a letter, he asked a small boy where the Post Office was. When the boy told him, Graham thanked him and said: "If you come to church this evening, you can hear me telling everyone how to get to heaven."

"I don't think I'll bother," the boy said, "You don't even know your way to the Post Office."

The mother of a four year old boy struggling to get him into a pair of leggings said: "James, lift up your legs." To which the child promptly replied: "We lift them up unto the Lord."

Zero hour was approaching as the small boy hurried on his way to school. "Please God, don't let me be late," he repeated over and over again. Suddenly he stumbled and fell. Picking himself up slowly, he muttered, "All right, you needn't push me."

The matron of a nursing home in Perthshire had her six year old niece visiting her. The little girl looked at a very old lady and said, "Are you very old?" After a pause the lady smiled and replied: "No, I wouldn't say that I was old, but I must admit that I've been young for an awfully long time."

A three year old who had had
enough of kneeling for what
seemed to him never-ending
prayers in church, got up
wearily and declared,
"Me knees are full!"

Sorry Bishop

A retired admiral gave a dinner party
to which were invited several
illustrious guests. His small
granddaughter was allowed to say
goodnight to them before she went

to bed. She went around the room
and eventually came to a bishop
resplendent in his purple robes.
"Oh," she said, "I do like your dress.
Do you have knickers to match?"

A little girl was out walking with her parents who belonged to a very strict sect of professing Christians. As they were walking, a donkey put its head over a gate and she ran to pat it. She exclaimed:

"Oh, Mummy, look! it must be a Christian donkey, it has such a long face."

When I was about nine years old, the raised garden of our house overlooked the local Roman Catholic presbytery garden. Looking over the fence early one morning, I saw one of the fathers pacing up and down with his hands behind his back. Being an inquisitive child I asked: "Father, what are you doing?" He replied "I have done something wrong and have to walk fifty times forward and back with peas in my shoes as a punishment." I said "The peas must be awfully hard." He grinned as he looked up at me and said "Don't tell anyone – they're boiled."

A rather scruffy little boy asked a very snooty church if he might join their Sunday School. He was told that they would consider it and was asked to come back in two weeks' time. When he returned they told him that they had not made up their minds. "Don't worry," said the

boy, "I no longer want to join."
"Why ever not?" they asked. "Well,"
answered the boy, "I have been
having a chat with God and he told
me that he has been trying to get in
here for years and hasn't managed it
yet."

From Australia – Dust to Dust

On the way home from church, a little boy asked his mother:

"Is it true, mummy, that we are made from dust?"

"Yes, darling."

"And do we go back to dust again when we die?"

"Well, the outside of us does anyway."

"Then, in that case," the little boy said earnestly, "I think there's someone under my bed, but I'm not sure whether they're coming or going."

A bishop was astonished to hear a little girl say that you had to be brave to go to church. "Why do you say that?" he asked. "Well, I heard my uncle tell my aunt last Sunday that there was a canon in the pulpit, the choir murdered the anthem and the organist drowned the choir."

A little boy attended a church service for the first time with his grandmother. When the collection plate was passed along the pew, grandmother put some coins in it. The little boy piped up: "I'm not five yet gran – you don't need to pay for me."

Little boy, to his minister:

"I don't pray every night because there are some nights when I don't need anything."

A Road Safety poster exhibited near a school read:

"Drive carefully past schools.
Don't kill a child"
Next day there was an addition
in childish scrawl: "Wait for a
teacher"